GOING WILD

Nature in My Backyard

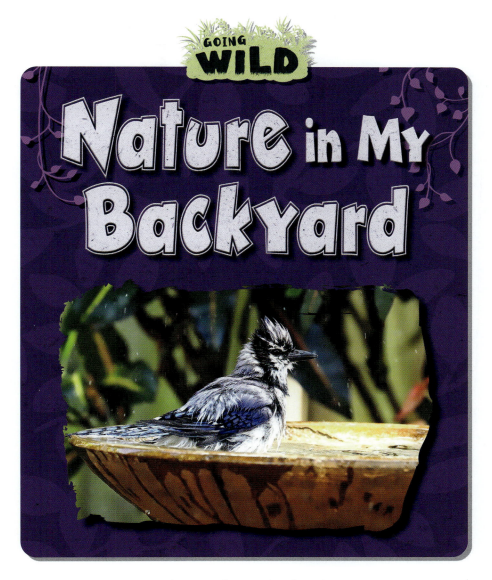

by Noah Leatherland

Minneapolis, Minnesota

Credits
All images courtesy of Shutterstock. With thanks to Getty Images, Thinkstock Photo, and iStockphoto. Recurring images – Very_Very, Barbara.M.Mattson, Apostrophe, ArtKio, Ton Photographer 4289. Cover – pashabo, WinWin artlab, Hibrida, judyjump, Milya Shaykh, Elena Platova. 2–3 – encierro. 4–5 – Galyna Andrushko, Teo Tarras, Damsea, LeManna, robert_s. 6–7 – Mongkolchon Akesin, Ground Picture, Martin Fowler, Jack Frog. 8–9 – Stock Up, eurobanks, Kay_MoTec, Susan Edmondson. 10–11 – Matee Nuserm, Andrew Angelov, Andi111, Sharon Epperson. 12–13 – BBA Photography, Elvan, Lois GoBe, Wirestock Creators, Wut_Moppie. 14–15 – Stephanie Braconnier, Media Marketing, GIOIA PHOTO, 1000 Words, Niki Florin. 16–17 – dvlcom - www.dvlcom.co.uk, Kristyna Henkeova, Studio.G photography, Johanna Poetsch, Sabine Seiter_sh, Martin Hibberd, dies-irae, Olivier Le Queinec. 18–19 – aRTI01, Lotus Images, James Andrews1, ALEXANDER KOLIKOV, Kristine Rad. 20–21 – William Edge, Lightspring, Evan Lorne, Electric Egg, Krisana Antharith. 22–23 – encierro, Lucky Business, kryzhov, Paul Maguire. 24–25 – Anastassiya Bezhekeneva, Lalandrew, Vadzim Mashkou, ITTIGallery, natrot. 26–27 – Ody_Stocker, kamilpetran, Dimaris, Aleksandr Rybalko, SpeedKingz. 28–29 – LeManna, oatawa, Monkey Business Images, SAKARET. 30–31 – Maridav, L. Feddes.

Bearport Publishing Company Product Development Team
President: Jen Jenson; Director of Product Development: Spencer Brinker; Managing Editor: Allison Juda; Associate Editor: Naomi Reich; Associate Editor: Tiana Tran; Art Director: Colin O'Dea; Designer: Kim Jones; Designer: Kayla Eggert; Product Development Assistant: Owen Hamlin

Library of Congress Cataloging-in-Publication Data is available at www.loc.gov or upon request from the publisher.

ISBN: 979-8-88916-974-1 (hardcover)
ISBN: 979-8-89232-151-8 (ebook)

© 2025 BookLife Publishing
This edition is published by arrangement with BookLife Publishing.

North American adaptations © 2025 Bearport Publishing Company. All rights reserved. No part of this publication may be reproduced in whole or in part, stored in any retrieval system, or transmitted in any form or by any means, electronic, mechanical, photocopying, recording, or otherwise, without written permission from the publisher. Bearport Publishing is a division of Chrysalis Education Group.

For more information, write to Bearport Publishing, 5357 Penn Avenue South, Minneapolis, MN 55419.

CONTENTS

Going Wild 4
Helping at Home 6
Water Worlds 8
Woodpiles. 12
Wild Gardens 14
Bug Hotels. 16
Bird Feeders. 18
Compost 20
Vegetable Gardens 22
Reduce, Reuse, Recycle 24
Carbon Footprints 26
Reducing Your Footprint. 28
A Better Future 30
Glossary 31
Index. 32
Read More 32
Learn More Online 32

GOING WILD

Nature surrounds us with dense forests, sparkling oceans, towering mountains, and rolling prairies. There are millions of different kinds of plants and animals that live alongside us on Earth.

Over the years, however, humans have harmed our planet. We have built over natural spaces to make room for farms, homes, and cities. Our factories and vehicles have polluted the environment with poisonous **chemicals** and **exhaust**.

Damage to the planet destroys the **habitats** of plants and animals.

All the different parts of nature are linked together. This means that damaging one part can damage other parts as well. At the same time, however, healing one part can also make a broader impact.

Humans need to work together to care for the planet and heal the damage we have caused. Everyone must do their part to help Earth stay healthy for future generations of plants, animals, and people.

HELPING AT HOME

People around the world are working hard to protect and **restore** nature. You can help, too. Each day, you can do a little something to support wildlife in your own backyard!

Help nature without ever leaving your home. Small changes can make a big difference to the plants and animals in your area. And this helps improve the health of the whole planet.

Have you ever noticed the sorts of wildlife living in your yard, garden, or community parks? If you don't find much in these places yet, don't worry! There is plenty you can do to help **attract** and take care of wildlife around your home.

Ask an adult before getting started. You will need permission and help with some of these backyard wildlife projects.

Water Worlds

All plants and animals need water to survive. But many lakes, ponds, or other watery homes have become polluted or destroyed. You can make your own wet and wonderful habitat for nearby plants and animals with just a few materials.

Ponds

You will need:
- A large **watertight** container
- A small shovel
- **Gravel**
- Stones
- Rainwater
- **Native** pond plants

- Find a spot in your yard that gets some sunlight and some shade.
- Bring your container to the spot you have chosen.

You can also dig a hole in the ground and add a pond liner to make it watertight.

- Use your shovel to dig a hole big enough for your container. You can also set your container on the ground.
- Place some gravel in your container. Add stones around the edge to make a way for creatures to climb out.

If your container is above the ground, place some stones around it so creatures can easily climb in.

- Fill your pond with rainwater or water from a nearby stream or lake. Tap water may contain chemicals that can harm animals.
- Add your native plants around or inside the pond.
- Wait for wildlife to find your new pond!

Butterflies puddling

PUDDLING STATIONS

Butterflies drink water from **shallow** puddles and wet soil. This is called puddling. You can make your own puddles for them.

You will need:
- A shallow dish or saucer
- Gravel
- Stones
- Soil
- Water

- Fill the dish with a mix of gravel and soil.
- Add some stones for the butterflies to rest on.
- Add enough water to make the soil very wet.
- Leave the dish outside near plants and flowers.
- Keep an eye out for thirsty butterflies!

In hot weather, you may need to add water if your puddling station dries out.

BIRD BATHS

Bird baths provide water for birds to drink and clean themselves. You can make one for your backyard birds.

You will need:
- 2 small or medium-sized clay pots
- A large clay saucer
- Strong outdoor glue
- Water

- Place one pot upside down on the ground.
- Stack the other right side up on top of it.
- Add a large saucer on top.
- Carefully glue these parts together. Let the glue dry completely.
- Fill the saucer with water.
- Watch birds fly in for a bath.

Be sure the bird bath is tall enough to keep other animals, such as cats, from reaching the birds.

11

WOODPILES

What is a minibeast? Think of small creatures, such as bees, butterflies, worms, snails, slugs, and ants.

Tiny minibeasts can play a huge role in nature. Some pollinate plants, helping them reproduce. Others help break down fallen leaves, dead trees, and plant and animal waste. They return the **nutrients** in these materials back to the soil, enriching it for new plants to grow.

Minibeasts often live in dead wood and leaf piles. You can gather your yard waste to create habitats for a community of tiny creatures.

You will need:
- Dead wood from logs, twigs, and branches
- Fallen leaves

- Find a shady spot in your yard.
- Pile up your pieces of wood.
- Add the fallen leaves around the bottom.
- Leave the wood and leaves to rot, and let all kinds of creatures make a home.

Sometimes, mushrooms or other **fungi** also grow on woodpile homes.

Fungi feed on dead wood, and snails and slugs feed on the fungi. Then, creatures that eat snails and slugs, such as squirrels, frogs, and turtles, may drop by, too!

Mushrooms growing on an old log

13

WILD GARDENS

WILDFLOWERS

Nothing brightens up a garden like colorful and sweet-smelling flowers. Native wildflowers are plants that can naturally grow in your area. They feed and provide shelter for local wildlife. When you plant them, you are giving a big boost to your community of backyard creatures.

Wildflowers are important for many different animals. Bees, butterflies, and other insects are attracted to their nectar and pollen. These creatures then attract other animals, such as birds and frogs.

If you can't grow a wild garden at home, ask a teacher if you can make one at school!

14

Even a small wildflower patch will make a healthy and inviting home for many creatures. The most important thing about growing wildflowers is making sure your garden is as natural as possible. So, be sure to check which wildflowers are native in your area.

WILD LAWNS

Your lawn can also go wild! Letting grass grow instead of mowing it creates habitats for many insects, birds, small animals, and flowering plants.

Bug Hotels

If you want to attract minibeasts to your yard, why not build them a hotel? Bug hotels are structures where many different creatures can live. You can buy one prebuilt or have some fun making your own!

Bug hotel

Building bug hotels can be a big job. Ask for an adult's help if you need it.

Bug hotels should have lots of small holes and cracks to attract all sorts of minibeasts. The hotels can be big or small. The best bug hotels are made from **recycled** or found objects.

You might already have lots of things you can use to build a bug hotel.

Find some pinecones and squeeze them together until they stick. Minibeasts will crawl through tiny spaces in the cones.

Pieces of bamboo can become homes for tiny insects.

Straw and hay make safe spots for minibeasts to sleep.

Stacks of stones can make cool, damp spots for frogs to rest.

Add a tile roof or cover to keep the hotel dry.

Bird Feeders

An easy way to keep nature healthy is to feed some of the wild animals that visit your yard or garden. Bird feeders can be a huge help when birds are struggling to find something to eat during the winter.

Sunflower seeds

Stores sell bags of mixed seeds, nuts, and fruit made to attract many different kinds of birds to your feeders.

You will need:
- An empty plastic bottle with a lid
- A stick
- Scissors
- String
- Birdseed

Ask an adult to help with the scissors!

Plastic bottles can make lots of different bird feeders.

- Use scissors to poke two holes through opposite sides of the bottle near the bottom.
- Poke the stick through the bottle, using the holes you just made.
- Make two more holes above both sides of the stick. This is were the birds will reach in to get the food.
- Poke two small holes near the top of the bottle and thread the string through them.
- Fill the bottle with birdseed and hang the feeder up with the string.

COMPOST

People sometimes use chemical **fertilizers** to help their yards and gardens grow. But these chemicals can be harmful to other parts of nature. They can poison the water and harm some plants and animals. A safer way to care for your yard and garden is with compost. This natural fertilizer is made of rotting plant parts collected from your garden and home.

Your plant and food waste can be collected in a compost bin in your yard. This material will break down more quickly if it is warm, moist, and gets lots of air.

Turning your compost with a shovel will help it get plenty of air.

WHAT CAN YOU COMPOST?

Not everything can go into your compost bin. Make sure you are putting only the right things in.

COMPOST

Grass cuttings
Uncooked fruit and vegetable scraps
Tea bags
Coffee grounds
Old flowers
Newspaper
Cardboard torn into smaller pieces

DON'T COMPOST

Meat and fish
Cooked food
Pet waste
Plastic
Milk
Cheese

Compost is ready to use on your garden when it is dark brown and crumbly. Just spread it over the soil. Worms in the soil will help to mix it in.

Putting the wrong things into your compost can attract mice and rats.

Vegetable Gardens

Another way to help nature is to grow your own food. Every time you eat something that you have grown, there is less pollution. This is because there was no waste getting the food to or from the store.

Vegetable gardens can be as big or as small as you like. You can plant them in your yard or inside containers.

Use compost to help your vegetables grow.

22

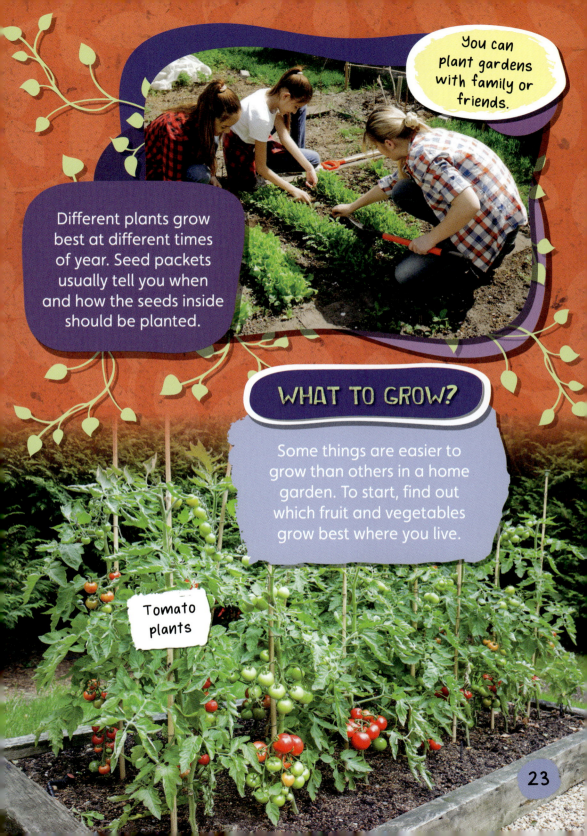

You can plant gardens with family or friends.

Different plants grow best at different times of year. Seed packets usually tell you when and how the seeds inside should be planted.

WHAT TO GROW?

Some things are easier to grow than others in a home garden. To start, find out which fruit and vegetables grow best where you live.

Tomato plants

23

Reduce, Reuse, Recycle

Every time a factory makes a new product, it creates pollution that ends up in the air or water. When we throw out an old product, we create garbage that piles up in landfills.

REDUCE

You can reduce how much waste you create at home by buying less stuff! Instead of buying water in single-use bottles, for example, just get one reusable bottle you can fill up many times.

24

REUSE

Think of ways to reuse old things. Maybe you could turn empty jam jars into handy storage containers. Try fixing broken electronics or learn how to sew and patch clothes.

RECYCLE

If you can no longer reuse, try to recycle. Recycling is using parts of things again so the materials they are made of don't go to waste. Paper, cardboard, aluminum, and most plastics can be recycled.

Look for this logo to see if something can be recycled.

CARBON FOOTPRINTS

WHAT IS A CARBON FOOTPRINT?

When we burn fossil fuels to power our homes, factories, and vehicles, we release a gas called carbon dioxide into the **atmosphere**. The gas acts like a heavy blanket, trapping in Earth's heat. The more carbon we add to the atmosphere, the warmer Earth gets. Rising temperatures are causing changes to our climate, making it harder for many plants and animals to survive.

A carbon footprint is a measure of the amount of greenhouse gases released as a result of a person's actions. The carbon dioxide released to make and ship a product is part of a carbon footprint.

Imagine a store-bought sandwich. The ingredients may have come from many farms and were shipped to a factory. Then, the ingredients were packaged and sent to the store, where they were made into a sandwich. By the time you buy the sandwich and drive it home, a lot of fossil fuel will have been burned for one sandwich!

All the carbon dioxide released adds to your carbon footprint. But there are some small changes you can make to reduce the size of your footprint.

REDUCING YOUR FOOTPRINT

Everyone has a carbon footprint. But we can make them much smaller by making some easy changes to how we live.

TRANSPORTATION

Most cars release carbon dioxide. For short trips, try walking or biking. For longer journeys, taking a bus or train with other people reduces everyone's carbon footprint.

FOOD

What people eat can affect their carbon footprint. Cattle farming releases a lot of carbon. Because of this, eating red meat makes a big carbon footprint. Eating less will help shrink your carbon footprint.

Cows also make a lot of another gas called methane. This traps heat just like carbon dioxide does.

CLOTHES

Buying new clothes adds to your carbon footprint. Just as with food, many different materials have to be shipped a long way to make clothes. All of this requires burning lots of fuel. Consider buying secondhand clothes from thrift shops instead.

29

A Better Future

Everyone can play a part in helping Earth. You can turn your corner of the world into a safe place for all sorts of plants and animals. Then, when you reduce, reuse, and recycle your waste, you'll shrink your carbon footprint to help the entire planet.

Grab your friends and family and go wild together! You might find out that they are just as ready to help the planet as you are.

Glossary

atmosphere the layer of gases that surrounds Earth

attract to draw the interest of something

chemicals human-made substance that can sometimes be harmful to living things

exhaust gas that escapes from fuel-burning engines

fertilizers things that are added to soil to help plants grow

fungi living things that feed on dead or decaying material

gravel small crushed stones

habitats places where plants and animals live or grow

native naturally found in an area

nutrients things needed by plants and animals to grow and stay healthy

recycled made from materials that were originally used for something else

restore to make something change to what it was like before

shallow not very deep

watertight sealed so that water cannot get in or out

INDEX

birds 11, 14–15, 18–19
bugs 16–17
carbon footprints 26–30
cars 28
clothes 25, 29
compost 20–22
fossil fuels 26–27
fruit 18, 21, 23
ponds 8–9
vegetables 21–23
wood 12–13

READ MORE

Benedetto, Carola. *Stories for Kids Who Want to Save the World.* New York: Seven Stories Press, 2021.

Feldstein, Stephanie. *Save Native Plants (Take Action: Save Life on Earth).* Ann Arbor, MI: Cherry Lake Publishing, 2024.

Tallamy, Douglas W. *Nature's Best Hope: How You Can Save the World in Your Own Yard.* Portland: Timber Press, 2023.

Walker, Tracy Sue. *Climate Change Activism (Searchlight Books—Spotlight on Climate Change).* Minneapolis: Lerner Publications, 2023.

LEARN MORE ONLINE

1. Go to **www.factsurfer.com** or scan the QR code below.

2. Enter "**Wild Backyard**" into the search box.

3. Click on the cover of this book to see a list of websites.